D1383684

SNAKES ALIVE

Kraits

by Ellen Frazel

BELLWETHER MEDIA • MINNEAPOLIS, MN

Note to Librarians, Teachers, and Parents:

Blastoff! Readers are carefully developed by literacy experts and combine standards-based content with developmentally appropriate text.

Level 1 provides the most support through repetition of high-frequency words, light text, predictable sentence patterns, and strong visual support.

Level 2 offers early readers a bit more challenge through varied simple sentences, increased text load, and less repetition of high-frequency words.

Level 3 advances early-fluent readers toward fluency through increased text and concept load, less reliance on visuals, longer sentences, and more literary language.

Level 4 builds reading stamina by providing more text per page, increased use of punctuation, greater variation in sentence patterns, and increasingly challenging vocabulary.

Level 5 encourages children to move from "learning to read" to "reading to learn" by providing even more text, varied writing styles, and less familiar topics.

Whichever book is right for your reader, Blastoff! Readers are the perfect books to build confidence and encourage a love of reading that will last a lifetime!

This edition first published in 2012 by Bellwether Media, Inc.

No part of this publication may be reproduced in whole or in part without written permission of the publisher. For information regarding permission, write to Bellwether Media, Inc., Attention: Permissions Department, 5357 Penn Avenue South, Minneapolis, MN 55419.

Library of Congress Cataloging-in-Publication Data

Frazel, Ellen.
  Kraits / by Ellen Frazel.
    p. cm. – (Blastoff! readers. Snakes alive)
Includes bibliographical references and index.
  Summary: "Simple text and full-color photography introduce beginning readers to kraits. Developed by literacy experts for students in kindergarten through third grade"–Provided by publisher.
  ISBN 978-1-60014-614-5 (hardcover : alk. paper)
  1. Sea kraits–Juvenile literature. I. Title.
  QL666.O64F73 2011
  597.96′4–dc22   2011004210

Printed in the United States of America, North Mankato, MN.

080111   1187

Contents

Kraits are one of the most **poisonous** snakes in the world. The common krait is one of the four deadliest snakes in India.

Kraits grow to be between 3 and 8 feet (1 and 2.5 meters) long. They have small heads and round eyes.

Kraits are gray, black, or dark blue. Many have yellow or white stripes. Some kraits have red heads.

Kraits have smooth **scales** on their bodies. The scales on their bellies are called **scutes**. Kraits pull on their scutes with strong muscles to move.

scutes

Kraits live in southern Asia. They make homes in grasslands, jungles, and forests.

= areas where kraits live

Their colors and patterns are good **camouflage**. They blend in with the dark jungle and hide in tall grass.

9

Kraits lay eggs in soil or in the **burrows** of small animals. They watch the eggs until they hatch.

Young kraits live on their own. They are born with deadly **venom**.

Kraits have few **predators** because of their venom. However, they do face other poisonous snakes.

The king cobra is one of the krait's most dangerous predators.

king cobra

Kraits rest during the day. They **coil** their bodies and hide their heads under the loops.

Kraits hunt at night.
They move quietly
in search of **prey**.

krait prey

Kraits hunt lizards, frogs, and rats. They often eat other snakes.

Kraits also hunt and eat other kraits. They are **cannibals**!

A krait bites prey with its small, hollow **fangs**.

Venom moves through the fangs and into the prey. It **paralyzes** the animal.

The krait opens its jaws wide to swallow the prey whole.

The animal is gulped
down from head to tail.
What a big meal!

Glossary

burrows—holes or tunnels in the ground made by some animals

camouflage—coloring and patterns that hide an animal by making it look like its surroundings

cannibals—animals that hunt and eat their own kind; kraits eat other kraits.

coil—to wind into loops

fangs—sharp, curved teeth; kraits have hollow fangs through which venom can move into a bite.

paralyzes—makes an animal unable to move

poisonous—able to kill or harm with a poison; the venom that kraits make is a poison.

predators—animals that hunt other animals for food

prey—animals hunted by other animals for food

scales—small plates of skin that cover and protect a snake's body

scutes—large scales on the belly of a snake that are attached to muscles; snakes use scutes to move from place to place.

venom—a poison that some snakes make; krait venom is deadly.

To Learn More

AT THE LIBRARY
Huggins-Cooper, Lynn. *Slithering Snakes*. North Mankato, Minn.: Smart Apple Media, 2007.

Jackson, Tom. *Deadly Snakes*. New York, N.Y.: Gareth Stevens Publishing, 2010.

Martin, Michael. *The World's Deadliest Snakes*. Mankato, Minn.: Capstone Press, 2006.

ON THE WEB
Learning more about kraits is as easy as 1, 2, 3.

1. Go to www.factsurfer.com.

2. Enter "kraits" into the search box.

3. Click the "Surf" button and you will see a list of related Web sites.

With factsurfer.com, finding more information is just a click away.

Index

The images in this book are reproduced through the courtesy of: Bruce Coleman, front cover, pp. 8-9; Ephotocorp Ephotocorp/Photolibrary, pp. 4-5; Stephen Reed, p. 5 (small); Michael D. Kern/naturepl. com, pp. 6-7, 11; John V. Owens, p. 7 (small); Jon Eppard, p. 8 (small); Jean Paul Ferrero/ardea.com, p. 10; David M. Dennis/Animals Animals – Earth Scenes, pp. 12-13; Omar Ariff Kamarul Ariffin, p. 13 (small); Sunil Sachi, p. 14 (small); Dhritiman Mukherjee/Age Fotostock, pp. 14-15; Shutterstock, p. 16; Mark Moffett/Getty Images, p. 17; Captain Suresh Sharma, p. 18; Paolo Gislimberti/Alamy, p. 19; Manoj Veerakumar, pp. 20-21.